Beyond the Shadow

Maggie Catchick-Houghton

Presentation by *BookLeaf Publishing*

Web: www.bookleafpub.com

E-mail: info@bookleafpub.com

ISBN: 9789357214001

First edition 2023

For my family - past, present and future

ACKNOWLEDGEMENT

We are all the product of the many interactions with those around us. I am no different. My friends, family, students, teachers, colleagues, neighbors, mentors, and even casual acquaintances all are a part of my craft. I have learned from all of you, and owe so much of who I am today to you all.

PREFACE

"How do you learn to spell?
Blood, sky & the sun,
your own name first,
your first naming, your first name,
your first word."

~ Margaret Atwood
from "Spelling"

Never Say Never

Never is a dangerous word.
It is a closed door,
padlocked gate,
barbed wire fence,
curling and threatening off to either side
as far as we can see.

But the secret is,
"Never" only has power
if we give it,
hang our heads,
kick at the door or shake the fence,
and walk away defeated.

For there is always a key to unlock any door.
Wire cutters and axes
can create an opening
where there once was none.
Even just walking around,
looking, pushing, digging,
might reveal another way.

"God always opens a window…"
Christians might say,
but really this goes way back

to the beginning of mankind.
It is in every mythology we hold so dear:

Orpheus storms the gates of Hades,
The Greeks find a way into Troy,
Scheherazade keeps her life,
and Jonah is spit back up on that distant shore
coughing, spitting, looking up to the sky.

Why I write

Words stretch,
reaching,
searching wide,
hoping to touch
the intangible,
and discover the truth
within the fictional.
Even the creation of
a monster
brings forth connection,
for there is
spirit,
breath,
soul,
in every life.
Words stretch,
reaching like a fog,
sliding slowly
around the heart.

The first time I knew
I was a girl

The first time I knew I was a girl
was when I wasn't allowed to sleep over
at my best friend's house
because he was a boy.

It was knowing
there were places I was not allowed,
places I would never be accepted.
It was knowing
what it is to be shut out,
to be looked at as different,
and somehow –
unimaginably –
dangerous;

for even then I could sense
there was more to that refusal,

something that could "happen,"
something forbidden,
and it would be my fault.

This was also the first time I realized
I had power.
Power that others want to control and lock up.
And it was the first time I wanted to go
where I was first forbidden.

Fading Away

I remember the dangling swings
on the school playground:
chains dusty with rust,
thick as a ten-year-old's finger,
black rubber seats – always warm,
riding those swings back and forth,
pumping our legs and straining
then leaning back into the endless blue
of a cloudless summer sky.

And I remember my friend,
a boy with hair so blonde it looked white,
blue eyes almost transparent;
we would laugh and play
and yet even then he was fading from us,
the wall of a blood vessel in his head
straining with pressure,
thinning until it burst.
He complained of a headache at dinner,
but by bedtime they knew
something was wrong.
I didn't want to think about how
he told his dad he was scared
as they drove him to the hospital.

Our teacher stood before us
military haircut, posture erect
unprepared for this battle.
He drew pictures in chalk of a
jelly-fish thing labeled BRAIN,
talked of comas and miracles;
still I couldn't understand that
he was gone but not dead,
simply fading away.

That same year, the elementary school
closed its doors,
burned and gutted by some kids
playing a prank with a smoke bomb.
They decided it wasn't worth fixing,
so we held classes in the gym until June,
and then were blown to other schools
like the white fuzz of dying dandelions.
Changes became rooted in my history
as I watched Father and Mother fall apart
and uncertainty made me as dizzy
as a merry-go-round that refused to stop.

After seven years sleeping alone
to the sound of his own heartbeat on the monitor,
the boy died, fading away from us at last.
At the funeral I smiled at our pictures,
kids in muddy jeans and jelly-smeared faces,

but couldn't look at the later photos
of an eighteen-year-old's body:
six feet tall, nurses shaving him daily
clipping fingernails
as his eyes wandered under their locked lids.
I didn't want to think about
what you might dream of
over seven years fading from life

What frightened me most
was the sight of our teacher,
a grown man, hiccupping through sobs
in front of a room of children;
how he kept repeating,
some things just aren't fair
some things we just can't explain.
And he was right.
But they happen anyway,
for not every sky will remain a cloudless blue,
and though we may chase after them,
we can never follow the dandelion seeds
once the wind catches them and whisks them
away.

Grasping at Straws

Who wouldn't cry
for the abandoned child?
Beggar in the streets?
Little match girl,
bare feet blue with the cold?

I never knew such hardship, it's true,
but it's hard not to feel abandoned
when parents choose another path over you.
Mother floating off on the bubbles in her wine
drowning in her own sorrows
lost to me beneath the waves
leaving me alone upon the shore.
Father eternally sailing away,
puffed full of the winds
that pull him away from me,
eyes searching the horizon
for warmer, palm-lined shores.

I know it isn't fair to them,
but even their deaths seem like
a personal affront to me,
another escape from my arms,
as ashes sink beneath the earth and waves,
and they continue to elude my grasp.

Where we belong

I'd like to fly,
but I am no bird.
I need to feel what I'm holding on to
the strength of a tree limb.
More like the squirrel
I jump as far as I can,
but always return to its steadiness,
feeling it bend beneath my weight
then snap back to where we belong.
For a moment I feel the rush
of air whistle in my ears –
but squirrels cannot really fly.

It is the movement I love,
scurrying from one branch to the next,
so long as I can keep my grip
on what sustains me:
rough bark and cool leaves that shade me
in the quiet spaces, dark between the green.
I can look out on all that is
but still be protected,
safe from the eyes of a hawk or vulture,
quietly drinking in the world,
while holding on tight to the branch
beneath me.

Ready to Learn

With the dropping of the leaves
comes the beginning of school,
and as a teacher, I enter excited.
It is a process like birth each year,
in the way that birth is like death,
endings and beginnings all woven together.
How fitting it lasts just nine months.

So I teach as they watch me,
and I learn as they speak to me,
looking back with quiet eyes
as I tell tales of the Faerie Queene
and mockingbirds,
of Pip's adventures, Carton's sacrifice,
and the days when Arthur was king.

They return to me, day after day.
The defiance of a dark-haired boy
leaning back in his chair,
daring me to teach him.
The dreamy idealism in a bright girl's eyes.
The sullen girl slowly chewing her gum,
more comfortable with calculus and trig.
The boy frantic with finding the meaning
hidden behind letters,

lines between his furrowed brows.
The girl I could have been. The girl I was.
The boy I dated. The dreams and
sorrows of the teenage years
I have almost buried,
the pressures and expectations
I haven't yet forgotten.

There is no meaning
in the mundane things in life
except this:
they are necessary and they continue,
filling the unthinkable gap
that would be left if they stopped.
So we go on – I go on – trying
to show the injustices of man-made monsters,
created and forgotten,
of Ozymandias, Big Brother, and pigs with a
five-year plan.
I challenge them each day to think on the
meaning of a Grecian urn,
truth and beauty like firefly concepts we can
bottle up and investigate,
of the passion and fire in a love like
Cathy and Heathcliff's,
a quivering butterfly pinned down for their view.
And they challenge me to teach them,
to reach them.
Daring me to ask for the best they've got,

fearing it won't be good enough,
telling me they don't care,
hoping I still will.

Until spring comes and our time together is over.
They are released to the beaches
and blossoming world
and I am left to wonder
if a seed has been planted.
Still, though I complain, I return
to the cycle, year after year,
always excited, always hopeful,
as we enter the first day together,
ready to learn.

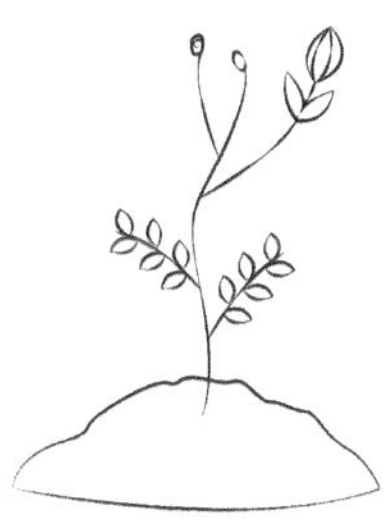

Mars is Calling

The Red Planet shines down,
bright among the distant stars,
and I imagine it casting a reddish glow
across the backyard,
peeking over the trees from the clear night sky.
The newscasters say Mars is as close
as it's been in years,
and I feel its pull, beckoning me from the
blackness –
air cool and crisp – and like Frost I
pause before those deep winter woods
and wonder,
What *could lie in wait for me out there?*
Would it devour me whole
if I surrendered myself to it?
Never to be found again…
The thought brings excitement rather than fear
and I force myself to close
the double-paned glass door,
returning
to the yellow glow of the kitchen lights,
and the steady hum of the refrigerator.
I sit and write with Mars to my back,
safe as a picture
on the other side of that door frame,
shut away behind the glass.

Primal Love

Quietly, I step into the silent room
allowing the darkness to envelop me.
Within this space, my children lie sleeping,
and in an instant, one million years of
civilization dissolves.
I am tense and alert, all senses and raw energy,
testing the air for unseen dangers lurking.

Listening for their heartbeats
falling into rhythm with my own,
I bend to smell their soft scent,
tasting their white skin
as I kiss their warm necks.
Tiny hands grasp at my hair, my fingers,
even in their sleep,
reaching instinctively.

And in this darkness, I know,
as we breathe one breath in unison,
that we are animal-fierce in our connection,
and the drum beats of their hearts
will always awaken in me a might
that would race howling into
blood, claws and fire.

The Silent Sentinel

Tall boy with dark eyes,
drawn to wild images
of shadowed Japanese ninjas
curved blades slicing
Japanese girls with wide eyes
too large, like a doll's
images he copied page after page
in sharp lines and
stark contrast, black and white
splashes of red on
       lips, wounds, the odd rose

He comes to my desk
gift in hand.
It is an Asian dragon
tiny statuette
mouth open, bearing fangs
tail curling in and over itself
       like a serpent in motion.

"This is for you. To protect you,"
he says simply, and I thank him.

It sits on my desk still,
a silent sentinel poised to chase away

demons that might surface
from where they hide in the corners –
        doubt, disappointment,
        rage, discouragement –
creeping forth when the day is done,
students are gone, and all is quiet.

My tiny dragon is there
to protect me.

And how sad that it is only now, when years
have slipped between us
that I pause to wonder…
        what demons so consumed
        that tall boy with the dark eyes
        as he drew his mouthless ninjas
        and girls with their wide eyes?

        And why did he choose me
        to share the gift
        of his protection?

Hope Pushes Through

I come to the garden with the weight
of my troubles on my back.
But it is a glorious mid-April day in Michigan,
and that is not to be wasted.
The crocuses are blooming,
hidden beneath rotting gray leaves of last fall
and I have to carefully pull the heavy
wetness away from where the
flowers have pushed right through
the thick mat of leaves,
giving them room for light and air,
room to grow and find the sun.

Life will find a way, as they say.
Even when bitterness, disappointment,
anger, and self-doubt lay their
blanket of smothering dampness down,
thick and rotting,
there is always something new
just waiting to push through.
So, today, I will help it out.

To Whom Does Grief Belong?

To whom does Grief belong?
Is it something as universal as the air, or water
raining down upon us and all nearby as well?
Can we soak it in, breathe deeply,
and know the depth of pain?
Can we sound its darkness?
Be baptized and born anew, forever changed
by the sobs and moans, anger and loss?

Guarding our privacy in grief
is my family's way,
cold and waspish in our desire to allow
only a select few
to see that soft, pink underside,
as if this makes us special or weak or strong.
When my grandfathers died, I was ten years old.
Deemed too young to attend their funerals,
My mother and father flew in separate directions
to grieve in ways I never witnessed or shared.
I was allowed to choose a souvenir
from their belongings
and told to remember,
but any questions were hushed.

And I learned, for when the call came,
announcing my own father's death
I didn't pick up the phone.
The hush of death surrounding his bed
in the hospice where he lay, seeped its coldness
through the blinking screen,
and I turned away, afraid of making a scene,
of making eye contact with his end,
taking my own time to prepare
for a new existence without him.
My step-mother folded in on herself,
at the center point
of the hurricane swirling,
proclaiming she alone could know this grief,
the rest of us with our childhood memories,
were merely feeling
the outer rings of wind and rain, a light,
peripheral damage.

But grief does not belong to her alone.
Death counts and obituaries scream
the grief in the world
as bells toll forth the loss and demand
that we listen and take heed.
Once in a grad class, on the very first day, an
Arab woman received a phone call
she took in the hall.
We were shocked when she burst
back in the room, wailing

that her father was dead, her father was dead,
>   *he's dead, dead, dead*
And we stared, paralyzed
by the public display of her grief,
a literal tearing of cloth and gnashing of teeth,
as she pulled her hair
wept and wailed like a wounded animal - pitiful
and dangerous.
One among us rose to pat her back,
rubbing in circles and murmuring,
there, there, who can we call?
>   *How can we help?*
But it was not I. I sat dumb and wondered
how she could be so open?
amazed by the honest display of emotions,
when I was too afraid to even pick up the phone.

The New Teacher

Watching her enter school,
I pause to see her.
My steps slow to match hers.
She is burdened by bags bulging with papers,
dragging a smart briefcase on wheels behind her
like a ball and chain;
shoulders slump under invisible weight,
hair, dusted with new-fallen snow,
is twisted back to help her look
older than her students.
After rummaging through her bag for keys,
she lets herself into her room.
Her smile to me is quick enough
to be called automatic,
but there is a crease pinched between her eyes.

I wander in and we chat
as she pulls out a stack of papers and sets them
on the one bare spot on her desk
between other towers of papers,
some leaning,
bristling with sticky notes and tabs,
others regimented into neat rows,
but no less daunting.

I know she is worried, ashamed even,
as she laughs about all the papers,
all the work to do.
All the work not yet done.
And I want to tell her, *it's okay, don't worry,*
But I know how hollow those words sound.
Like an accusation even,
as if worrying is just one more thing
she might be doing wrong.
So I say nothing, but nod and smile
and groan with her,
hoping it's enough.

Just then, the students begin to enter,
and as I fade back
I watch her grow and the light in her
begins to glow and shine forth.
The students are drawn to the light, I can see.
They flutter around her with news questions
about homework and schedules,
jokes they heard, and book titles to share.

As I slip out the door,
Leaving her with her wide smile, smooth brow
to the students who need her,
I know that this is what matters.
I remember that this is what has carried me
through my many years.
I pray that she can see her own value

before the light is smothered
by heavy blankets of doubt and expectation.
And I hope that I can continue
to protect my own tiny flickering light
for those who flutter forth
in search of some warmth.

SMART goals

The school requires goals
that are Specific, yet Measurable,
Attainable, Results-focused, and
Time-bound. So,
my students' test scores will be
their guide and the evaluation
of my teaching effectiveness
this year, disregarding
any other more valuable evidence.
They will stretch my students
into pie charts and pin them down
on data lines and graphs
performing the mathematical calculations
necessary to find out
what they will believe about me.

But I have a secret.
For within my heart
I have created another set of goals
that are so Vague as to have vision;
Immeasurable for they seek more
than can ever fit into a bar graph;
they surpass what is attainable,
for what is Possible is what I seek,
no matter how improbable the success;

and rather than results-focused
they are goals which may never
see a result at all.
These goals are about a Process –
creating a spark, tossing a pebble in the pond,
the flutter of the butterfly's wings –
and these goals will never know
the explosion, widening rings
or vast hurricanes they have created
for it may take centuries to become.
So, you see, my goals are not time-bound
nor test-bound, nor bound in any other way
for it is the Unbound freedom of education
I seek:
seeds in the black earth,
dandelion spores blown to the wind.
They are waves upon the ocean
and the unending cycle of the river
on its path to the sea.

These are my secret goals:
To hear my students, when they speak
and when they are silent
To honor their lives, struggles, choices,
successes, challenges, and creations
To challenge them to see new ways of looking at
the world…
to hear new voices from lives unknown to them
to smell, taste and touch the world they live in

to know that now is what matters
to feel deeply what is important to them
To walk with them on a path that is neither
smooth and easy, nor safe and familiar, but to let
them know that I am with them, and they can do
this – even if they think they can't
And, most of all, to teach my students what is
TRUE:
> You are amazing and powerful
> You will change the world
> All you have to do to succeed is believe
> And you are more than any number

In the end, when the numbers
and data are calculated and filed
and my students move on to their future lives,
we will see how effective a teacher I have been.
And it will have everything to do
with the goals I have set
and the work I have done to achieve them.

Recess for Everybody

I want to live in a world where
Recess doesn't end with elementary school.
Where well into high school
students break two to three times a day
to go outside and play
baseball and touch football;
tossing Frisbees and batons with abandon;
diving with racquets in hand
to swat the tennis ball, shuttlecock or
racquetball.

And teachers don't just stand in clusters
watching, either.
They spin circles, singing,
"Ring around the rosie!"
or chase each other in spirited games
of duck, duck, goose and tag.
In the courtyard, one turns head over heels
doing cartwheels until she cannot stand straight.

And this mandated time for play
extends well beyond our schools
to the world of work and industry.
Men in business suits leave a
crumpled pile of double-breasted jackets behind

as they sail through the air,
loosened ties streaming behind them,
to dunk and block and shoot and rebound.
Women kick off high-heeled shoes
and spin hula-hoops or jump hopscotch.
"Men at Play" signs announce the situation
as construction workers
laugh and slide by the side of the road
avoiding a dodgeball.

It would go so far as to reach Washington, D.C.
and become commonplace to see
Senators joined together, holding onto the edges
of a giant parachute billowing over their heads;
or Congress playing kick the can,
while on the White House lawn
calls are heard of "Red Rover, Red Rover!"
And somewhere on the Mall,
between men and women squealing as they
dodge and dart through sprinklers,
are the Supreme Court Justices,
robes flapping wildly around them
as they spin a complicated pattern of rope,
jumping in and out and over with glee!

Finding You

"When you feel the mist on your mouth and
sense ahead the embattlement, the long falls
plunging and steaming – then row, row for your
life toward it" ~ Mary Oliver from *West Wind*

There was so much danger
in finding you,
in upsetting my little world
into the dark depths of possibility
lurking beneath me,
that I almost failed to look about
and see how small things had become,
how cramped the spaces,
how my muscles ached from remaining
contained.
I can tell myself now that it was
self-preservation and fear,
but there was laziness and complacency too,
and pride in self-sacrifice masked as
self-control.
We are all programmed with life-preserving
instincts
until Love!
Love is the biological override.
For love we leap into the ocean,

brave the raging river rapids,
shriek back at the storm,
and descend into the depths,
lungs bursting for want of air.
Because even greater was my want of you.
So, for the sake of love,
we pick up the phone,
open the door,
pause in the street
waiting just to see
if he'll turn back again.
For love we give up
every notion of who we are,
who we were, and
who we are supposed to be,
just for this one chance to see
who we might become.
We row, row for our lives
towards the falls and this one chance
to fly.

The Necessary

Heat seeps out of your body
and I breathe you in,
your skin salty sweet with sweat,
I kiss your shoulders, neck, and thirst for you.
Basking in your arms,
legs luxuriously entwined,
wrapped in you,
I feel the rise and fall of the earth
knowing this is The Necessary.

What Matters

There is a boy
who occupies my mind
when I think of
the matter of Black lives.

Tall, young,
skin the color of the earth after the rain,
well-built, a football player, hair cropped close,
wide bright smile, but never given easily,
one must earn that smile
and when given, you know it matters.

He has a beautiful name with African origins,
takes great pride in that and its originality,
no matter that I know someday it may
keep him from interviews or jobs.

This is a young man becoming a man.

He has good parents
and to him their thoughts matter.
Tells me, "alright if I bring home a C,
but better not have no missing assignments."
They do not want him to miss any opportunities.

When the national anthem is recited
he remains firmly seated in class,
but slowly and deliberately
rises for the moment of silence after.
When the school tells teachers we must stand
in the halls to greet each student as they enter,
he soon takes up a place beside me,
greeting them also, many with their own
individual, intricate handshakes.

I know he has integrity.
I know he has a good heart.
But will these things, however important,
matter to the world?
His height and build will lead them
to see him as a man,
but he is still very much a boy
and only just got his license.

He told me
one morning there was a shooting on his block,
how he walked past the yellow tape
to the school bus,
the neighbors already gathered and watching,
excited and nervous.
When I said, "That must have been scary,"
he tucked his head and gave a quick "yeah."

One day in class he exploded,
angry with another student,
loud and cursing,
he hit desks and knocked a chair over.
When I told him to take a walk,
he left with the door slamming behind him,
yet when I found him later on a bench in the hall
he was in tears
at the ferocity of his own emotions.
He couldn't express to me what was the matter,
"Just a bad day," he repeated,
and when he returned to class
he shook hands with the boy
who was and is a friend to begin with,
but with anger like this,
someday there may be trouble.

He wears his pants slung low,
though I remind him daily to pull them up,
flat-brimmed baseball cap
I remind him daily to remove,
Airpods in his ears,
though he knows they must come out.
It is a daily ritual with us.
I remind him,
"This is school, these are the rules."
He makes me remind him
to remind me:
This is who I am.

I calmly say the words each day,
And he carefully takes off
the trappings of his world
to join mine.
No disrespect – it is our nod of greeting.
Together we say, *I see you.*
But there are others who will demand he stoops
to enter their domain.
They think they are teaching him The Way,
but do not acknowledge there is another way,
and for this there may be trouble.

They refuse to see what matters.
This is a boy who matters
to me, to his parents, his life matters
and to the world he could be a man who matters,
but when I consider all that is
the matter with this world
I am left only with fear and concern
as I consider the Black life ahead of him.

On the Edge

You call us edgy
because we live on the edges
where we were pushed from your center stage.
We learned to make the edges
our own
and now you fear what you
can only see from the corners of your eyes.

You have called us witches and worse
and we are All you have made us out to be
for we learned there is more truth
in what is left unsaid
hanging in the silence
more Comfort in what we create
over hot flames and feed
to hungry souls to fill them with warmth;
there is more Power in spells we sing
to children on the edge of the night
to lull them to sleep
in the incantations we write and read
and write again
to bring others to new worlds,
and what dreams may come.

We are marginalized
and so we have learned to live in the margins
like annotations, finding insight
as we see inside your carefully printed words
beyond even what is written
to what may be, might be, and is.

We are "she" and "he" and "we" and "they"
but never You.
For you broke with our gaze
and refused to look us in the eye
so now you must fear what you would not see
for We feel no need to stoop to explain
nor twist ourselves into the tiny box
of your understanding.

We fly because we have wings
and we shine with our own light,
here on the edges
an aurora dancing in the night sky
beyond your reckoning

We are as strong as water
that swallows boulders whole
and seeps into the cracks and edges
to burst them apart from within
strength of the silent sea, waiting,
that surrounds the land

We are fall and spring -
a riot of death and rebirth
the colors and smells of blossoms
and rot and rich earth
fire red leaves which Burn crimson
before they fall

We stir the pot as you told us we must
turning the mixture within, toil and trouble,
though you recoil from the swirls and eddies
brought to the surface

We make the homes as you told us we should
but you shudder when the homes we create
are in our own image and not yours

We see All around us, color & darkness,
forgiveness & revenge, comfort & torture,
control & freedom,
for we have lived all these dualities and know
there is never one without the other
here on the Edge
the line between two realities
a tightrope to be walked

You sit squat in the center of your middle
and believe the earth is flat
but we have gazed beyond the edges
to the bend of the horizon

and new days beyond,
breath flowing in and out
day's end and beginning

We lather ourselves in all of it, rinse and repeat
for this is our world on the edge,
the one you refuse to see,
and the view is wild and spectacular!

Seagulls in Flight

I love to watch seagulls in flight
as they glide upon cushions of air
hanging suspended between heaven and earth
floating on nothing.

Their calm arching peacefulness
brings to mind artist's paintings,
the splashes of white high above the sea
standing out against a cold, gray sky.

I think I could love seagulls
if only they would stay that way.

But I know too well what happens
when they land:
the screeching and squawking as they fight,
viciously greedy over a bit of fish guts
they scrounged from the garbage-strewn sands.

Beyond the Shadow

Beyond the shadow
of a doubt
lies the blaze of Certainty,
a shining, glowing state,
difficult to look at from
here in the darkness.
And though I may step to its edge
to be seen by others as
capable, calm, collected, controlled,
I know I am anything but.
For I prefer the comfort of my doubts,
the variations of light and dark
that play in these shadows
and the possibilities that lie
in not knowing
for certain.
Within the shadows of
my doubts
I may retreat, reside, reflect and ruminate,
for at least I know here
I am never alone.